A Poetry Novel

EXIST WITH ME

CLEO SANCHEZ

© Cleo Sanchez

All rights reserved. No part of this book may be used or reproduced in any manner whatsoever without the written permission from the author except for the brief quotation in a review.

Cleo Sanchez
www.typewriterandmoss.com

*"You are allowed to be both a masterpiece
and a work in progress simultaneously"*

-Sophia Bush

Prologue

Narrated in one of my favorite movie, <u>500 Days of Summer</u>, is the line: "You should know up front, this is not a love story."

I feel as though this quote perfectly encompasses the extent of this poetry novel.

This is *not* a love story. This is a journal of my thoughts, successes, and obstacles during heartbreak.

Within the context of the book, I am the protagonist and the antagonist all at the same time. Expressing my thoughts through poetry and prose has allowed me to share my voice, in which I once believed to have lost in my former relationships. Nonetheless, I have found my voice again, but it swears like a sailor.

I am utterly and unapologetically, human.
Exist with me.

You set me on fire,
And I ended up apologizing
For burning..

When you should have burned
For me too.

Part One

I look at him
And I don't even see *him* anymore.
I don't see the same man I dated
Three and a half years ago.

Hell, I'm not even sure
If I consider him my best friend.

I enjoy his company,
But his voice.. his tendency to lie..
And skillful wording…
It makes me want to vomit.

The bullshit. The lies.
Is this really what I what I've got to keep living for?
Is this my life as his wife?

I'm not sure if this is what I want anymore.
Our marriage feels like I have a mold growing
Inside of me…

From my broken heart,
To the rest of my organs,
Filling my lungs.
This love is killing me.

Thank you
For sparing me
The stress
Of us ever having children.

Thank you
For being
So careless,
So I could find your infidelities.

Thank you
For helping me discover
That I had the confidence
To finally leave you.

Everything in life is a choice.
Anything he chose to do
Was his own choice.

And this relationship?
There will be a choice
If I am perceived to be an *option*.

Because I am *not* optional.
I deserve to love, and be loved.

This time feels real.
I'm ready to finally leave.
I'm no longer ashamed,
To share how he treats me.

He was supposed to love me,
Unconditionally.
Why did I deserve this?

My mind wanders dangerously
In waves of self doubt.
Am I unlovable?

You blamed your infidelity on me.
I was always so busy,
So inattentive to your needs.
You described me as always pissy.

Did I even make you happy?
Or did you just want me,
So you could display me
As a trophy?

I was nothing short of a prize,
One that you had thrown away,
Despite all my cries.

In Mexico,
You showed me different parts of you.
You became more vulnerable,
Showed off your family, too.

Why did you select parts of yourself
To share with me?
Even though we made a vow almost four
years ago..
You were never honest, my little pin.

Your family called you Pinocchio.
Pin, for short.
Your lies were longer than
That large nose of yours.

You did what was comfortable,
For you.

You loved and cared for me,
But you *wasted* my time
Not knowing what you needed
To care for you.

At first,
I blamed myself.
I wasn't sexy enough
To keep you faithful.

I offered solutions,
Bought new lingerie,
Yet, you still never changed.
You were always unfaithful.

When I finally stood up for myself,
And wanted to leave our marriage,
I tended to you while you were sick,
You were still unfaithful.

You never took accountability.
Your lies seethed through your teeth.
You never took accountability.
Not even when you put your hands on me.

And yet, you still deny everything.
Why?

You knew what you did
Was so damn wrong.
I wanted you to leave,
But you begged to stay.

You begged so damn much,
That you were willing
To sleep on the floor,
To just be by my side.

Pathetic.

Your voice used to be like poetry,
So beautiful.
So warm.
It felt like home.

Listening to your voice now
Feels like nails on a chalkboard.
It makes me cringe
And my eyebrows raise.

It's funny what betrayal does
To your mind.
You're no longer my home,
And I no longer have anymore fucks.

Your reality is so distorted,
That you still believe,
Despite the truth and evidence,
That you are a *good guy*.

I gave you a small spoonful
Of your own medicine,
But you'd rather tell everyone
That I poisoned you.

It will be the liquor,
And the resurfacing of
Your blanketed lies
That will end up making you sicker.

When she blasted you on her Instagram story,
It was the *truth*.

It wasn't once,
It wasn't twice,
It was the whole damn time.
I even told you how much it bothered me...

It didn't phase you. You owned that title.
You didn't even try to change.
You never followed through,
Your words meant nothing.

You played me so well.
Please accept your throne, king.
But I will not be at your side,
Fuck your monarchy.

You sit on
A throne of secrecy,
Sexual addiction,
And gaslighting.

Oh god,
You played it so well.
For far too long.
I'm so glad I'm gone.

Because fuck your monarchy.

Your excuses became your bible.
You believed every ounce of pain
You brought me was righteous.
But every action was so selfish.

You lived to hurt me,
You showed no remorse.
Your actions allowed me to see
That you truly were,
Narcissistic.

Your smile, your charm
It fools everyone.
I see through it now.
Every past action
Glares in my face
A bright, red alarm.

He fucked me up so bad,
And now I'm searching
For a love
That I'll never have…

Please leave me
The fuck alone.
I'm left broken.
I can't pick up my pieces.

I can't stop drinking,
And numbing my pain.
Self sabotaging with many men,
To feel some sort of blame.

You know..
I didn't even like you at first?
You carried yourself with arrogance,
You chain-smoked and heavily drank.

But slowly over time,
I felt a magnetic energy from you.
A force so powerful that
I felt a glimmer of attraction, too.

There was still something off
I ignored all of the signs.
Even when I discovered your infidelities,
All of the seven times.

I don't like who I am,
When I'm alone,
or when I'm online.
I seek validation.

Maybe it's because I don't
Really feel seen
when I'm the most me.

I've lost myself,
Seeking everyone's approval,
When what truly matters most,
Is supposed to be me…

He hardly told me he loved me
And actually meant it.
He said it quickly in passing...

But it was in the important moments,
When I needed to feel loved,
That I wasn't told I was.

He told me he loved me,
But continued to mistreat me.
It's becoming clear
he was never *the one.*

Who the fuck do you think you are?
Please don't mistake my kindness for
weakness.

Because of you,
Now my heart is filled with darkness,
So much *deepness*.

It would have been so much easier,
If you would have just died.
Because the damage you caused,
After you lied..

I can't change the way
That it has made me feel.
But you don't seem to care,
Won't your two-faced mask just finally peel?

In the wake of your destruction,
I'm left here.
Stranded, alone.
No one to help me cheer.

Because the damage you caused,
After you lied..

In so that it seems,
It would have been so much easier,
If you would have just died.

I miss him.
I miss the attention.
When we flirted.
Played hard to get.
Fingers barely touching.
Remembering each others' scents.

I always felt like he could hear my heart.
Feel how fast it was beating.
For him.
Can he hear me?

But then,
Over the years,
It just stopped.
He stopped giving me attention.

And gave it to others.
As if I wasn't here anymore.
But I'm still here.
Can he hear me?

Whiskey on your breath,
Your body hovering over me.
My body trembled with fear,
Red was all you could see.

You can't keep me anymore,
I'm not your trophy.
Even after you were served the papers,
You clearly couldn't see.

I had to let you go,
You kept making decisions for me.
And I thought moving on to someone new,
Would allow you to finally see.

Seeing red,
you pressed your thumb up against my neck,
Left me gasping for air.
I wished I were dead.

Will you finally let go of me?

It's revolting,
How even through it all..
You seem to believe
That you did nothing.

Refresh your memory,
Because quite frankly,
My dear, you aren't Shaggy.
You can't claim it wasn't you.

The charges on our bank account,
The messages to girls from college,
Female coworkers, hell— even my friends..
You sure it wasn't you?

Forgetting important dates
On Christmas and Valentine's Day..
I wish it was fucking fake.
You sure it wasn't you?

And the worst dismissal of it all?
The moment you saw my parents at the bar,
You pleaded that the bruises you left,
Weren't from your arms.

Did hurting me
Make you feel better?

When I chose to leave
Our toxic marriage,
Did you finally realize
That I was what you wanted?

Or did you just enjoy
The thought, the idea..
That you could be
with someone else.

You wanted it all.
You wanted me for comfort.
You wanted thrill and adventure,
But never asked me for it.

When you cheated on me,
Year after year.
I blamed myself.
Did it make you feel better?

All that's left
Of us, our love…
is now a restraining order.

I'm searching for whatever love
I can reach,
Because you never
Gave it unconditionally to me.

The only passion
You ever gave,
Was when your hands were
Wrapped tightly around my neck.

You set me on fire,
And I ended up apologizing
For burning..

When you should have burned
For me too.

I'm packing away my life.
A new beginning.
A fresh start.

But packing it all away,
and throwing out the memories,
reminds me of that day..
of what went wrong.

When in reality,
Our love wasn't that strong.

We were two broken people,
Living broken lives together.
One where we didn't share
What actually gave us pleasure.

You've broken your vow.
Too many times.
You're just becoming
a distant memory now.

I'm packing it all away.
You're only a memory,
I'm going to be okay.
This is a fresh start.

Part Two

The true depths of my despair,
Are only seen by the far few..

I hardly like to tell a soul,
Of the disgusting truth.

I choose who I let in,
My heart is timid and weak.

What do I do
When I'm depressed?
Eat leftover pizza
For breakfast.

You're sweet,
But I'm damaged.

You don't want me.
You just want the idea of me.

You don't know what I battle internally
Every waking day.

You just want the pretty blonde
With the smile.

But I'm damaged.

Today I let you in.

Your smile felt familiar, so safe.

But as the night ends,
I'm reminded of the pattern.

When I get too close,
They run away.

And when I choose to fight or ignore,
Those ones want to stay.

Then I pull out my journal,
And write poems from the pain.

The night of our first date
Plays in my mind
Like a broken record.

It felt like a scene in a Hallmark movie.
I'm absorbing every memory
Of it all.

The glances across the small table,
Lost in your eyes.
You are sensitive, inclusive..

Im intrigued.
It felt like a bubble was around us,
Not even a breath
Or a whisper
Could burst that moment of intimacy.

You drove me home,
And I asked you to stay.
The whispers of the pool
Called our name.

You didn't bring a swimsuit,
So you bravely jumped in.
The water embraced you,
As you later embraced me.

Curled up in your arms,
Our lips as wet as the water,
We couldn't let go
Of one another.

The sky soon became covered,
In a light cloud layer.
Lightning flashed above us,
As we kissed in the water.

His presence is magnetic.
He makes me feel alive.

I would have never gone for him,
He's not really "my type."
But what even is "my type" but just a list
Of admirable physical qualities.

He's a person,
With a courageous soul.
And indeed—
Suited in chivalry.

I know I need to end things.
It will never work out.

We're polar opposites,
And I suppose that's
Why I was drawn to you.
A *magnet*.

I guess in the irony of it all…
I always knew it would never work.

We haven't ended things yet,
But I can already feel the end.

And it will be me,
Not you…
Left not standing.

So I'm ending things.
Because I can't stand the thought
Of being hurt.

I crave his touch.
I crave our hands grasping
For one another,
In embrace.

I crave his kisses,
His longing looks.

You are a sex god,
You make me feel liberated.
I can do anything,
And you love every bit of it.

You can't get enough of me.
I make you feel young.
But man, oh man,
You are a sex god.

I had to convince myself
The last time we had sex,
That it meant nothing.
We were only friends.

All the pecks of kisses,
On my shoulder,
My neck,
My forehead.

Nothing.
They meant nothing.

Just the same way,
That it meant nothing
When you held the door for me,
Held my hand.

The way you fed me
Across the dinner table,
And shared your food.
It meant nothing.

We are nothing,
Not even sure if
We can call each other
Friends.

If you wanted me,
You could have had me.
I'm no longer waiting.
You blew your chance.

In the chaos of it all,
I still want you.
Even though I am nearly damn sure
That you don't want me.

You don't reach out.
It shows that you don't even care.
Not even a little bit,
Not even at all.

I'm just your plaything.
Your late night call.
This time… this time,
You've dropped the ball.

That inch of attention,
That I try to justify as love,
It's not enough anymore
I won't wait for your call.

Delete my number,
I don't need your inconsistency.
I won't allow myself
To feel incredibly small.

I craved intimacy
So badly
That I didn't fully listen
To your communications.

Are we even meant to be lovers?
We are so incredibly wrong
For one another.

Despite our age,
Our careers,
Our hobbies,
I didn't care.

I craved the way
You made me feel.
Our passion.

I think I'm finally
Starting to see,
You did share.
And it hurt you too much.

Because at the end,
Of it all,
You also did seem
To truly care.

It's been three months,
Of hopelessly
And utterlessly
Waiting for you.

I need to let you go,
For me.
So I can finally have
An ounce of sanity.

I compared the last few
To you.

It wasn't fair of me,
To have that mindset for each of them.

They never held the door for me,
Continued witty banter..

With the others,
I was searching
For that spark to replace
The fuse I once had with you.

Is it possible to fall
In love with others
So suddenly?

Or is it because
I lacked the love..
The attention..

That when I finally received,
It felt foreign to me..

You sat on the edge of your bed,
Strumming your guitar.
I sat down next to you,
Thinking about how the whole night was bizarre.

You are so attractive.
Years ago, I wanted you.
But as I sat there pondering,
I just wanted the vision of you.

As I'm sure you only wanted the same of me too.

I'm only trying you on
Like this season's hottest dress
Right off the rack.

I'm only trying you on,
To see if you fit.
You don't.

I'm only trying you on,
And it was pleasant for a moment.
I was hoping it would fit.

You're just a stranger now,
A stranger
That knows
All of my secrets.

Your love and attention
Made me feel safe,
And now the thought of our end,
Cuts me the *deepest*.

I saw you in my dreams again,
I know it's time to let you go.

The memories of you,
Will slowly dissipate.

I hope that in all of my art,
You will know.

I've always loved you.
Even though, you are no longer my soul mate.

Three glasses of wine,
And all I keep thinking about is you.

Boy, you are so fine,
Do you think of me too?

I felt lonelier
When I was
In bed with him,
Than I do now.

It gets better.

I want my "Eat Pray Love" moment.
Where I fully embrace
Who I am
Where I've been
And immerse myself
Fully into the present.

I want to find that balance,
Of life and love..
Where loving myself
Comes first.

Part Three

Why does it feel like I'm not enough?
I am enough.

Why does it feel like I'm not capable of being loved?
I am capable of being loved.

Why is it so hard to find unconditional love?
I deserve unconditional love.

I've got a shit ton of problems,
And as much as a I try,
Mediocre sex isn't going to solve them.

For many months,
I used men.
I used them as if
They were a renewable energy source.
They came and they went,
As fast as wind.

They always come back..
whether it's days,
months…
Men are always so damn predictable.

I was once a sexual prowess,
I laid my eyes for the kill.
I hunted them so quickly,
Each body gave me an initial thrill.

I was finally free,
I truly believed I was in my prime,
That after all of the years,
This was my awakening time.

I could do whatever,
And whoever I want.

Sex was the bait,
It gave me a sense of pleasure.
To reel each one of them in.
Intimacy became a lost treasure.

I only wanted to take control,
To temporarily displace the pain.
Erase the memory of him that night,
Because I never want to feel that way again.

The thought of home
Is lost.

Where is my home?
I call three different places
My home..

When it used to be
With you.

I don't want love
If it means
Sitting across at a restaurant
On each other's phones.

Not giving each other
Attention, Conversation,
Ignoring each other's needs..
I don't want a love like that.

I'm not easy to love,
I'm easier from a distance.

Because when they get too close,
And see the depths of me..

I'm too much for some.
Do I dare to love again?

Replace feelings with tattoos?
Or whatever my horoscope said.
I don't make the rules.
Hell, if I even follow them.

My independence is as bold as
The color on my lips.
The world is my playground,
That I happily relish in.

I follow passion and pleasure
Like a moth drawn to a flame.
A flight ticket purchased on a whim,
Adventure calls my name…

I lived most of my adulthood,
Believing that I was never good enough,
When in reality,
I was more than enough.

He wanted less,
But I will never be,
Anything but,
The absolute, fucking best.

I can't bear to love another,
Not now, anyways.

It's my turn to love myself.
I'm making up for lost time.
Almost a whole damn decade.

I am somewhere between
Kicking ass and taking names,
And desperately needing
To take a nap.

Only dead fish go with the flow.
They swim upstream.

Call me a fucking fish,
I never did follow expectations.
I'd rather scream.

I run with the damn wolves,
Feisty and free.

I am becoming the woman of my dreams.

I can't think of anything
more badass than traveling solo.
What better place than New York?

I dreamt of this moment,
As a little girl
Watching the shows
In the city.

I wanted to write,
I wanted to live
In a tiny apartment
in the city.
What happened to those dreams?

Being alone,
In a city
Filled with thousands of faces,
Felt cozy to me.

I wanted the poetry readings
In intimate venues,
I wanted the rainy days
Watching the street cars.

I fucking did it.
I made it happen.
All on my own.
I am the woman of my childhood dreams.

I'm turning my heartbreak
Into delicate pieces of art.

Learning to love myself first,
Is the start.

Because it was a pleasure
To love you,
But it was even more powerful
To start loving myself.

A whole year
Without you.
And yet, I am still
whole.

I have a life
Without you in it
And to me,
That now feels like home.

What lies beneath
Those deep, brown eyes
Is a mountain of strength
And the warmth of a bear.

You don't know
How handsome you are,
The way you push back
The curls of your hair.

And that little smirk
on the edge of your lips,
Twinkle in your eyes,
With so much love and care.

What a plot twist you were,
My dear…
I didn't expect to love you,
But now we are here.

You feel like the warmth of the sun
On a cold January morning.

I could get used to this.

I am healing,
Continuing to grow,
But damn does it feel good…
To trust and know.

I am happy,
Free,
Always learning.

And I've stumbled upon a person,
Who looks at me,
As whole,
A new version.

My past and scars
Are not an obstacle.

I'm given an abundance of love and strength,
But ultimately…
I hold the master key
To my heart

Exist with me.

Acknowledgements

First and foremost, I'd like to thank my mother for listening when I felt like I did not have voice, and my father for allowing me to find the strength to rebuild. To my grandparents— without your patience and wise advice, I would not have been guided in the right direction. I am so fortunate to be loved and supported by you all.

To Madison, Alyssa, and Maryssa— thank you for offering an ear, a glass of wine, and encouragement as I broke my silence and found myself again.

To those that inspired this book— you know who you are. Thank you for breaking my heart. The pain taught me that I am fully capable of loving myself, as well as how to be a better lover to others.

To my readers— Thank you for believing and trusting in me. Without your love and support in my endeavors, I would have not had the courage to share my story. I hope this book inspires you to create yours.

To my inner child—you fucking did it. You went to New York all by yourself. You wrote a book. You're living your dream, kid. Keep doing big things.

Consciously,
Cleo

About the Author

Cleo Sanchez is a business owner and creative soul from
California, who has received a bachelor's degree in Liberal Studies from California State University Sacramento.

Cleo is the owner of Typewriter and Moss, a small-town boutique in Northern California that focuses on curating and sharing local artisans. Cleo is also the co-owner and founder of The Exchange, a pop-up marketplace that showcases local artisans on a larger scale seasonally.

Cleo's first self-published book, "Exist With Me" is a collection of poetry and prose inspired by her battles in divorce, modern dating, and self love. Cleo enjoys traveling alone, reading books, treating herself to a warm bath, and drinking a glass of wine.

www.ingramcontent.com/pod-product-compliance
Lightning Source LLC
Chambersburg PA
CBHW022021290426
44109CB00015B/1258